"I³ is filled with powerful truths about the life of a leader—spelled out, inspirational, and easy to read. I've known Dan and his family for years. I watched him grow up in the mission and Christian publishing community. No wonder he has such good stories to tell, filled with wisdom and experience in leadership. Now that he is the President of Bethany International, I know Dan to be a man of integrity, loyalty, and commitment—a leader who knows God, His Word, and people. I happily commend Dan and I³ to you."

LOREN CUNNINGHAM ~ Founder of Youth With A Mission and International President of the University of the Nations

"Dan is the kind of man I want in my ' fox hole.' He artfully weaves three critical areas of life—identity, integrity, and impact—into thirty days of very relevant, real life stories that deal with everyday issues of leadership and life. The principles and truths are timeless treasures that you will find yourself reading over and over again."

BOBBY NORMENT ~ CEO of Rivendell Worldview Educational Company, LLC and Rivendell Sanctuary

"How refreshing it is to see a devotional book revolving around character issues. It is especially so at this time in our culture when these issues are being downplayed or neglected. I cannot think of a person who would be better qualified than Dan Brokke to speak to these issues.

"I have had the joy of working beside Dan for most of his adult life. He played a key role over a number of years in the development and growth of Dayspring Greeting Cards. He, with other team members, did what he could to implement kingdom values and integrity into every aspect of the business. It was Dan who put into action his words, 'Let's do everything we can to make our customers successful.' These types of statements reflect the character of Dan Brokke and the way he approaches family, ministry, business, and life. You will enjoy and be deeply blessed in the reading of this book."

DEAN KERNS ~ Co-founder of DaySpring Greeting Cards

"Since 1985, I have been privileged to know Dan Brokke as a worship leader, teacher, business consultant, mentor, and friend. He has relentlessly pursued his relationship with Jesus and never shrunk back from speaking the truth in love. Dan holds several key places on the highlight reel of my life where his advice, his correction, and his unconditional acceptance helped to transform me into a lover of God. Now, Dan is offering his wise counsel to many through this practical, relevant devotional. I highly recommend this for professionals, church leaders, and teachers for their personal edification and preparation to change their world."

STEVE SNEDIKER ~ Instructor of Cinema,
Visual Arts Department, John Brown University

"A book that is illustrated by a rich life is a true jewel. For about thirty years I have had the privilege of working closely with Dan Brokke. Our relationship includes ministry, business, and family life. I have read his life and now his book. These devotions are slices of real life that embody great truths. Dan has lived them and is now passing them on to us. I have seen Dan demonstrate that no matter where God places us we are called to be servants and ministers. If there is one word that comes to mind when I think of Dan Brokke, it is integrity. Read these devotions to discover integrity and other valuable truths for yourself. You will be edified."

DON LEETCH ~ Co-founder of DaySpring Greeting Cards

IDENTITY > INTEGRITY > IMPACT

DEVOTIONS *for* LEADERSHIP & LIFE

DAN BROKKE

summerside
PRESS

I³—Identity, Integrity, Impact © 2009 by Dan Brokke

ISBN 978-1-935416-28-9

Cover and interior design by Müllerhaus Publishing Group, www. mullerhaus.net
Edited by Marilyn Jansen

Published by Summerside Press, Inc., 11024 Quebec Circle, Bloomington, Minnesota 55438
www.summersidepress.com

Summerside Press™ is an inspirational publisher offering fresh, irresistible books to uplift the heart and engage the mind.

Printed in the United States of America.

DEDICATIONS

To Dona
My wife and best friend…who continues to capture
my heart and build confidence.

To Harold and Cathy Brokke
My dad and mom…whose unconditional acceptance,
wholehearted love for God, and faithful example gave
me a joyful love for life—now and forever.

To Paul
My brother for 13 years…whose zestful life and untimely
death helped me know that my life is not my own and that
today's choices matter.

To Dean Kerns and Don Leetch
My mentors in business and ministry…whose humble
pursuit of the Kingdom of God and doing the right thing
in every choice and every relationship has become my
definition of leadership.

ACKNOWLEDGEMENTS

First, I would like to thank Jason Rovenstine, creative director for Summerside Press, for his encouragement to put into writing some of our discussions from the past years. And to Carlton Garborg for opening the door for me to share with others what has been in my heart.

Second, thanks to my wife, Dona, for making space for me to write. Even after leaving the responsibilities of home life on her shoulders for a week while I traveled, she still gave me the time and support to hide away and put thoughts on paper when I returned. Also, thanks to my children, Danielle and her husband, Mark (and of course Asher my grandson), Drew, Derek, and Dustin, who all bring me so much joy and are constantly in my heart. They are the biggest reasons to live an I³ lifestyle.

And what can I say about Marilyn Jansen, my editor? She saw the vision for I³, adopted it as her own, took what I gave her and made it more…made it better…and made it come to life. She wouldn't let me get by with sharing concepts without life examples. Her patience (and persistence) helped me overcome my tendency for procrastination.

Thanks as well to the countless friends through the years whose lives, choices, relationships, and partnerships shaped my thinking and convictions. I think of Dean, Don, Darrell, Sned, James, David, Bill, Randy, Drew, Phil, Michelle, Larry, Ruth, Cliff, Reba, Bobby, Jean, David, Diane, Loren, Dick, and the list goes on. These are the people who inspired greater leadership, expanded the scope of influence, and opened doors for continued impact. All are I³ people.

And finally, I say "Thank you" to my Savior and Lord. His patience and persistent love keep drawing me to Him. He has delivered me from myself time and again. His Spirit teaches me and makes the words of the Bible come alive.

CONTENTS

⋯> INTRODUCTION

After I graduated from college in 1976, my wife and I expected to go overseas for mission work. While my wife was getting her RN training, I began working at DaySpring Greeting Cards—an assignment that lasted twenty-four years.

My years at DaySpring busted the doors off of my expectations. Through my parents and as a child of God, I had always had an instinctive sense of "Christian" destiny—that I would live life as a Christian because of who I was. At DaySpring I realized that living that life was a choice, not a destiny. It wasn't circumstantial, but intentional. I discovered there was a difference. I saw in every task of business and in every relationship the overarching purpose was to know God and demonstrate His Kingdom—His indwelling presence—to the world around me. I grew in my sense of identity and calling.

It doesn't matter what line of work you are in, what position and title you carry, or what role you have—parent, friend, pastor, president, mom or dad—God does not separate between the sacred and the secular. In the Old Testament there were priests, prophets, and kings—each anointed for a unique role. When they acted in faith and in obedience to God's direction and ways, the fame of God spread throughout the nation and to neighboring peoples and nations.

God has always had an intense interest to live in a daily and intimate relationship with us. To show us the depth of His love, He did something that continues to mystify human understanding—He sent His one and only Son into the world as a baby. Into a humble woman's body, He planted the seed of Jesus who was to be the Savior of the world.

The impact of this one Man of integrity and faithfulness changed the course of human history. Jesus knew His true identity. He lived it with integrity. And the impact of His life, death, and resurrection brings hope to all humanity. It was, however, never His intention to do all this on His own. In the Sermon on the Mount, Jesus sums up the focus of our pursuit, "Seek first the kingdom of God and his righteousness, and all these things will be added to you" (Matthew 6:33 ESV).

The first step in living an impactful life for God's kingdom is to find our identity in Christ. It is through Him that we discover how God "wired" us—for what purpose we were created. The next step is to live true to that purpose, to grow in skill, depth of conviction, and in healthy relationships. We are to grow in character so that the evidence of our lives impacts people, drawing them to Christ. This is not about perfection; it is about pursuit. No one is sinless, blameless, and without fault...but we can still be people of integrity.

Jesus laid the foundation for *I³* living and leadership. He said, "I can do nothing on my own. As I hear, I judge, and my judgment is just, because I seek not my own will but the will of him who sent me" (John 5:29-31 ESV). He was totally free of fear because He walked completely in the light of His Father.

I³ is a devotional journey that seeks to encourage the alignment of personal experience with the Word and truth of Scripture, leading to transformational impact. I encourage you to use these chapters for reflection, sharing at work, small group growth, and processing life situations and needs. And, I pray that you will find joy and freedom in following Jesus' way, His truth, and His life.

DAN BROKKE

"We are God's workmanship, created in Christ Jesus to do good works, which God prepared in advance for us to do."

Ephesians 2:10 NIV

"You can spend your time scribbling and playing, or you can lead according to God's purpose."

CHAPTER 1

WHY EVEN BOTHER?

Who Cares If a Leader Is Godly?

⋯> IDENTITY

Like all young parents, we were learning on the job with our first child. Our daughter often surprised us with her statements and actions. She was nearly three, discovering her growing independence, and testing us when we experienced a memorable "contest of wills" moment. She was again refusing to obey us. In our frustration we asked her, "What would you do if you didn't have parents?" She replied immediately and innocently, "If I didn't, then I would just scribble and play."

In a simple way she captured why we need godly leadership—without it there would be no direction; no help in defining boundaries; no one to stimulate learning; no growth toward being a caring, Christian person; no fulfillment. Everything would be governed by urges to "play" at life, not live it. Danielle didn't think through all that, but she did understand our role as her parents: to be the leaders in her life and to enforce her boundaries.

⋯> INTEGRITY

Let not the wise man boast of his wisdom
or the strong man boast of his strength
or the rich man boast of his riches,

but let him who boasts boast about this:
> *that he understands and knows me,*
> *that I am the* LORD, *who exercises kindness,*
> *justice and righteousness on earth,*
> *for in these I delight.*

JEREMIAH 9:23–24

How well leaders play has become more important than how well they lead. Personality and charisma have become society's measuring stick for leaders. Our society stands in line waiting for the newest spin, scandal, or scheme. If this is what is expected, why even bother trying to be a godly, moral leader?

The Word of God has given us eternal standards and wisdom to guide every aspect of leadership. We are told that every choice, every action, every value, and every outcome will ultimately be measured by Jesus—that we will stand before Him to give account for what we did and how we led. All our choices matter—the public and the private ones. Did we live and lead by eternal standards and truth or by our society's ever-changing values?

When God created our world and us in it, He did so with purpose in mind. His first instructions were to "be fruitful and multiply." He wanted us to grow, to enjoy, to increase; and "to have dominion" over every living thing. He wanted us to rule, govern, and care for the world He made. He gave us the framework for leading with integrity, and it has nothing to do with looking good in the tabloids. It has to do with kindness, mercy, grace, justice, patience, and just plain "doing the right thing."

⋯> IMPACT

So who cares if a leader is godly? You might be surprised. Do not underestimate the power of one godly life to lead and influence others. You have a world of influence like no one else—in education, government, media, or entertainment; in homes, churches, work environments, or the Starbucks line. Within these areas of influence, how you live and how you lead can change lives. You are called to be a part of God's eternal purpose. You can spend your time scribbling and playing, or you can live and lead according to God's purpose. How the headline reads is up to you.

Are my values coming out of my own opinions or based on Jesus and His teaching?

Where do I have areas of relationship that influence others?

Is my influence godly and positive? Where is there room for improvement?

"The call to leadership and influence is fundamentally a call to serve."

CHAPTER 2

FOLLOW
THE LEADER

Leading Through the Servant Door

⋯> IDENTITY

My father is a teacher at heart. I have had the privilege of watching from a front-row seat as he has taught by example. In his quiet way, he is a leader of men. Through the years, many people have looked to him for guidance, sometimes without him even knowing it. He leads by putting others before himself and encourages young leaders to do the same.

When Dad turned 80, one of his followers wrote him a poignant note. It summed up the impact of my father's life: "Thank you for your faithful demonstration of leadership and for pouring yourself out in service to others. Thank you for being my mentor.... Later when our roles switched, you followed with respect and dedication. You showed me that leadership starts with servanthood and ends with servanthood."

That note was a testament to my father's greatest strength as a leader: he led through serving. He wasn't afraid to open the door to God's leading, even if it meant he was to follow another.

···> # INTEGRITY

The Son of Man came not to be served but to serve, and to give his life as a ransom for many.

MATTHEW 20:28 ESV

Without question, Jesus is considered the greatest leader in history. He continuously modeled the "called to serve" leadership attitude. The apostle Paul wrote that "your attitude should be the same as that of Christ Jesus: Who, being in very nature God, did not consider equality with God something to be grasped, but made himself nothing, taking the very nature of a servant" (Philippians 2:5-7). And it's true. Jesus chose obscurity, came into a humble setting, resisted claiming any position of authority, and went from village to village serving the hurting, the sick, and the oppressed. Ultimately, He chose death, carrying the sin, sickness, and pain of humanity.

The call to leadership and influence is fundamentally a call to serve. When we hear the word "leadership," the immediate impression is of someone who has power and positional influence. But Jesus rarely called a person to a role of leadership. Most of the time He would say things like "follow Me," "lay down your life for your friends," "lose yourself," and "be faithful in little things." Leading is sacrificing for others, putting others before self.

In the Bible, the mother of two of Jesus' disciples came to Him with a gutsy and self-serving request: "Grant that one of these two sons of mine may sit at your right and the other at your left in your kingdom" (Matthew 20:21). The other disciples, upon hearing what she had asked, were quite incensed. Jesus quickly stepped in and set things straight: "The rulers of the Gentiles lord it over them, and their high officials exercise authority over them. Not so with you. Instead, whoever wants to become great among you must be your servant, and whoever wants to be first must be your slave—just as the Son of Man did not come to be served, but to serve, and to give his life as a ransom for many" (vv. 25-28).

When I think of those who have most influenced my life, the greatest effect was not the exercise of their positional authority, but rather the example of humility and service to those around them. It is their "servant heart" that has impressed me.

···> IMPACT

There is perhaps no greater need than for leaders to be motivated by serving. By laying down their lives and leading by example, they are opening the door to godly leadership. The calling to serve is a calling to live like Jesus—to give our lives "as a ransom for many." Are you ready to make your big entrance into the world of leadership? Look for someone to serve.

When did I first feel the call to serve as a leader?

Where am I serving? Can I do more to serve there?

What leaders have I seen lead by serving? How can I emulate that leadership?

_____

_____

_____

_____

_____

_____

_____

_____

_____

*"Leaders often fall or rise based
on the strength and vitality
of their relationships."*

CHAPTER 3

NO MAN IS
AN ISLAND

Relationships Make the Man

···> IDENTITY

The story of the prodigal son tells of a boy who selfishly demanded that he receive his share of his inheritance *now*. He informed his father that as soon as he had the money, he would be leaving home to pursue life on his own. Amazingly, his father complied with his request. So off he went. Over the next few months, the young man lost everything. He ultimately found himself alone and dying. Miserable, he decided to go back to his father and humble himself, to ask for forgiveness and become like one of his father's hired men. In this moment of humility, he found restoration. His relationships were renewed, and he began to live again.

I don't know about you, but I have felt the pain of a broken relationship. At times I've waited way too long for the other person to make the first move or have avoided them altogether. When this happens, there is a sense of death and emptiness. I typically press through the hollowness by staying busy or diving deeper into activities. Eventually, however, I have to go to the other person, humble myself (even if I wasn't at fault), and express my desire to renew a vital, healthy relationship.

For husbands and wives this is common. How many of our emotional "backpacks" are loaded down with unforgiveness, selfish acts and attitudes, proud resistance, or resentment? We all seem to have a chip (or block) on our shoulders, waiting for our partner to repent. Is it any wonder that life and energy can be drained out of our world?

Healthy relationships—right relationships—are key to productive and life-giving environments, whether as a part of a family, a church, or a business. When I invest in and keep healthy openness with those in my world, I am more complete.

⋯> INTEGRITY

This is love: not that we loved God, but that he loved us and sent his Son as an atoning sacrifice for our sins. Dear friends, since God so loved us, we also ought to love one another.

1 JOHN 4:10–11

Do you ever feel alone, defeated, in need of renewed relationship? Do you feel like a deserted island that no one wants to visit? Are you waiting for someone else to act and take responsibility for your relationship? For someone to sail his boat over and rediscover you? God didn't wait for us; He came into our world to heal our broken relationship before we even asked.

We are not made to live in isolation. God made us to interact with others. In reality we all come into each relationship with legitimate human needs: the need for security, for achievement, for affirmation, and for unconditional love. Every person has a longing to experience and know healthy, intimate, life-giving relationships.

Leaders often fall or rise based on the strength and vitality of their relationships. As a friend noted, most people fail in their work not because of a lack of skills, but rather an inability to effectively function in relationships. Henry David Thoreau wrote, "An organization is the shadow of a man." If a leader is a "taker," an environment is created where everyone has to make sure they get their share, and the mentality becomes one of survival. If, however, a leader is giving and serving, a generous culture grows and thrives. Everyone receives from the top. They feel part of something that has meaning.

⸬> IMPACT

No man is an island. Our souls hunger for relationship.
Developing those relationships, helping people meet the
needs in their lives—that can be the making or breaking
of a leader. What are your relationships saying about your
leadership?

*Am I looking to others to meet my needs? How are others looking to meet
their needs through me?*

*Are there relationships in my life or organization that are being neglected?
What can I do to invest into those people?*

*In what two important relationships can I begin to serve? What have I
received that I can give?*

_____

_____

_____

_____

_____

_____

"Our acceptance of someone else is not based on the virtue of my goodness and forgiveness but rather on what Christ Jesus has already done for me."

CHAPTER 4

ROCKY ROAD IS NOT JUST A FLAVOR

Accepting Others for Who They Are

⋯> IDENTITY

I have a beautiful wife. We have been married for more than thirty years and have four wonderful children. She is my best friend. The recent years have been the happiest of our lives, and we love being on life's journey together. But it wasn't always so.

It didn't take long after marrying my wife for me to discover that she is a strong woman who doesn't just take my word for things. And she soon discovered that I have a tremendous ability to procrastinate. Throughout our years of marriage, there has been a lot to deal with—children, financial struggles, job changes, moves across country, friends going through crises, and uncertainty about the future. There were years when the road was so rocky that we were walking single file, not hand-in-hand.

At one point, life had gotten extremely tense. My new consulting business had demanded change and attention; switching from a corporate situation to being a freelance consultant had been stressful and tested us deeply. We were making it financially, but there was always an underlying uncertainty about our future. It is easy to accept each other when external circumstances and conditions are stable, secure, and predictable. During seasons of change like this, however, acceptance isn't as easy.

There was one particular morning when we broke through the tension to a place of unconditional love and acceptance. After twenty-five years of marriage, we were struggling. On this particular morning, however, our hearts were knit together at a deeper level. After spending hours in conversation the night before, we were finally able to embrace each other as God made us, accept the circumstances that shaped us, and forgive each other's failures. Our commitment became stronger than ever before. We vowed to never turn from the other and to always love the other—unconditionally. That acceptance cleared the path and transformed our relationship.

···> INTEGRITY

This is my commandment, that you love one another as I have loved you. Greater love has no one than this, that someone lays down his life for his friends. You are my friends if you do what I command you.

JOHN 15:12–14 ESV

We live in a fickle culture. There is so much attention on physical appearance and doing what feels good that people move in and out of relationships like they switch TV channels. If they don't agree with the other person, if the going gets tough, they move on.

Ultimately, however, all lasting relationships must come to a place of contentment and acceptance. The road may be rocky, but it's that journey that bonds us. Healthy, committed relationships generate life. Severed relationships lead to death. Something dies in us when there is a break in a relationship. When our relationship with God ends or we fail to hold up our side of it, the thing that dies is our spiritual life.

My standing with God is not based on my good works, but rather on what God in Jesus did for me. His forgiveness. His acceptance. His commitment. This is not only the basis for my relationship with God, but also the basis for my relationship with others—family, friends, colleagues, employees.

When we lay down our lives in humility and forgiveness for someone else, we are following Jesus' lead. He did it for us so that we could do it for each other. My acceptance of someone else is not based on the virtue of my goodness and mercy, but rather on what Christ Jesus has already done for me. He already took the penalty for all of our failures. That is the basis for moving past our personality flaws, failures, disappointments, and sins. It is the basis for moving into humility, forgiveness, acceptance, and love. It is the basis for a foundation of integrity and impact that takes us over the rough spots.

···> IMPACT

We all want to avoid the rocky places. We are tempted to ignore, deny, or even run away from conflict. Truly effective leaders, however, find ways to smooth out the rough spots. They build relationships with forgiveness, acceptance, humility, and perhaps a bowl of Rocky Road.

What are some reasons I have broken relationships?

How can I move in humility and forgiveness to bring restoration and healing?

In what ways can existing relationships be strengthened through greater acceptance and commitment?

"Our destiny, calling, and meaning in life flow out of our ability to adapt our will to God's."

CHAPTER 5

IF I HAD TEN YEARS LEFT TO LIVE...

Changing Priorities to Match God's Purpose

⋯> IDENTITY

A few years ago, I was asked to lead an organization that I loved. I had been in business leadership and consulting for more than thirty years. It seemed like everything I had accomplished had prepared me for this appointment. From that experience the normal approach would be to develop a formal process for this company with a vision, strategy, and plan, and then to work that plan.

Even before receiving this leadership role, however, I had begun to sense the need to "listen for God's direction, agree with Him, and then act in obedience." Now, this is a plan of sorts, but it was quite different in method from how I would normally have approached leadership. I used a "process." This new direction was essentially a plan to align with God's purposes and methods and then move forward with perseverance. That is not always easy, but I felt that it was how God wanted me to lead.

Over the next few months, I continued to ask God for His direction and listened when He gave it. His direction came through the wisdom of trusted friends, through the hundreds of emails I received, through prayer, through time spent in the Word of God, and in the correcting and confirming peace sent by God. The Holy Spirit illuminated His will and direction as I listened, read, and discussed the issues. The agreement of our board and leadership regarding this new direction gave us the confidence to make hard decisions, change the way we did things, and to carry on—even when things didn't go as anticipated. There was a sense of freedom and fulfillment in this kind of action. It led to unexpected success.

···> # INTEGRITY

I keep asking that [God]... may give you the Spirit of wisdom and revelation, so that you may know him better. I pray also that the eyes of your heart may be enlightened in order that you may know the hope to which he has called you, the riches of his glorious inheritance in the saints, and his incomparably great power for us who believe.

EPHESIANS 1:17–19

When the disciples asked Jesus to teach them to pray, the first thing He said was that we should ask the Father, "Your kingdom come, Your will be done on earth as it is in heaven." Aligning our identity with God's ways and purposes is the greatest way to discover who we are and what

path we are to take. It is the key to growing in confidence in
our lives and our leadership.

The truest sense of purpose comes from personally
inviting God to work in our lives to bring fulfillment and
eternal significance. Our destiny, calling, and meaning in
life flow out of our ability to adapt our will to God's. This
alignment shifts the responsibility for results from us to
God. He is responsible for the big picture. Our purpose
begins when we ask for a "revelation" of His eternal
purposes. Our impact begins when we follow the path
He reveals.

···> IMPACT

A while back, two key mentors in my life began to ask
themselves, "If we just had ten years left to live, would we
keep doing what we are doing?" At the time, they were
pastors of growing churches. The answer turned out to be
"no." They left their pastoral roles, to the shock of many
around them, and began to print and distribute messages of
God's hope. This led to the founding of DaySpring Cards.
Literally billions of Christian messages have touched people's
lives because these two men dared to follow God's purpose.

If I had only ten years left to live, would I keep doing what I am doing?

What has God placed in my heart through the years? Have I buried it, ignored it, or disobeyed it?

How can I begin now to move in the right direction to fulfill that desire...that good purpose?

_____

_____

_____

_____

_____

_____

_____

_____

_____

_____

_____

"Titles really don't matter. Freedom comes when we let them go, even if it means we have to eat a bit of humble pie."

CHAPTER 6

HUMBLE PIE

The Importance of Emptying Yourself

⋯⟩ IDENTITY

I was chaffing on the inside after about a dozen years of working in the corporate world I was in. I loved the work, but felt like I should be given more responsibility. It wasn't that I hadn't received a lot of freedom, opportunity, and responsibility. Frankly, I simply wanted more. The greed didn't consume me, but it was always there below the surface, affecting my attitude.

One morning I knew it was time for a long prayer walk. These walks usually have a pattern: pour out my heart (and sometimes complaints) to God, recognize and admit my personal responsibility, and finally surrender to God's ways. On this particular "walk," I complained that I should have been given more direct authority in leadership (and the title to go with it). Then I became convicted. I realized I needed an "attitude" of humility and service like that Christ Jesus modeled. I needed to surrender my pride. I confessed. Then I wrote in my journal, "I will serve whether there is any additional recognition or position given." There was an immediate sense of rest for me.

A co-worker and I were traveling some months later when he commented that he had noticed a positive change in our "atmosphere." Although the situation had nothing to do with him, he had recognized the change. He commented how it was now easier to be around me. Laying down my ambition and embracing a different attitude changed the environment and was noticeable in the very atmosphere of our workplace.

···> INTEGRITY

Your attitude should be the same as that of Christ Jesus: Who, being in very nature God, did not consider equality with God something to be grasped, but made himself nothing, taking the very nature of a servant.

PHILIPPIANS 2:5-8

This passage is thought to have been a song of the early church. It captured the essence of what it meant to be a follower of Jesus. He was not only the supreme example of how to live and how to lead. He was not just a person to emulate. He was the *source* of the attitude we are to possess. The early church saw that apart from the Spirit of Jesus, it was impossible to live like Jesus. He possesses the right attitude, and we enter into that attitude as we surrender to and find our life in Him.

Empty and make yourself nothing. There are few things more difficult than restraining your greatest strength and abilities when you know that you could fix something, lead more effectively, or provide the answer. For 33 years Jesus functioned in the confines of His human body—content to meet the needs of a broken humanity as a servant. He had the power to lead a revolt against the Roman occupation of Israel. In fact, all Israelites were looking for their deliverer, their Messiah. I'm not sure I could have resisted rising up to that place of leadership—but Jesus did. He had made Himself nothing for the sake of a higher and more redemptive plan—one that would cost Him everything.

Let go of your "inner castles." Our human nature is to gravitate toward the place of greatest identity, confidence, and trust. Jesus learned to trust His heavenly Father's will, ways, works, and words. He didn't hang onto His natural source of security (His own abilities and divinity) but rather embraced the identity of a servant. It is hard for us to let go of titles and recognition. We gain so much confidence from the labels we receive in life—teacher, manager, coach, vice-president, or supervisor. But titles really don't matter. Freedom comes when we let them go, even if it means we have to eat a bit of humble pie.

···> IMPACT

Surrender to God's will and work. It is such a simple phrase, "let this attitude be in you...," but it is so hard to do. We don't "let" much happen in our lives without some say in what it is and how it is done. We want to be in control. Emptying ourselves is not something we do lightly. Surrender goes against the ego and identity of any person. Yet it is what we must do if we are to have the attitude in us that was in Christ Jesus. It is what we must do if we are to have a godly impact on others.

What rights do I hold on to that get in the way of relationships?

Inner castles are places in which to hide. What titles, positions, and places of security do I hide behind?

How can I begin now to embrace the mind of Christ and walk in humility?

_____

_____

_____

_____

_____

_____

_____

_____

_____

_____

"Discovering purpose is not so much a process of growth as it is an awareness of what is truly important."

CHAPTER 7

STOP THE MADNESS

Surrender to God's Direction

···> IDENTITY

I have recently gained a new friend. He joined our organization after many years of successful leadership. He is in every way respected and trusted. His life is guided by the most remarkable sense of purpose.

More than twenty years ago, Tim and his wife Char had a daughter. Soon it was discovered that this dear little child was seriously handicapped mentally and physically. Well-meaning friends said they should put her into an institution. It was a very difficult time in their lives.

While trying to find ways to cope, they rediscovered the ninth chapter of John—the story of the man who was born blind. In this story the disciples asked Jesus for the cause of this man's blindness: "Rabbi, who sinned, this man or his parents, that he was born blind?" Jesus replied, "Neither this man nor his parents sinned, but this happened so that the work of God might be displayed in his life." Jesus went on to heal the man by putting mud made with saliva on his eyes and telling him to go and wash in the pool of Siloam.

Tim and Char came to believe that God had given them a gift. They began to pray that God would be glorified through Amanda's life, that others would be blessed through her, and that she would know just how much God loves her.

I recently met Amanda and witnessed how well she was loved by her family. It is difficult for her to communicate, yet I was struck by the joy she expressed in hearing a worship song and by just being with her family. She is loved. She blesses others with her joy. God is glorified through her and her family. There is a depth of character—identity shaped by suffering—and realness that touches the heart of anyone who sees them interact.

INTEGRITY

We constantly pray for you, that our God may count you worthy of his calling, and that by his power he may fulfill every good purpose of yours, and every act prompted by your faith.

2 THESSALONIANS 1:11

Our culture disposes of things that are inconvenient. Millions of babies are aborted, children are left to fend for themselves, families are abandoned for the job, and even well-meaning men and women are so preoccupied that they are often followed by a trail of broken relationships.

How can we stop the madness? There is a quiet voice calling us to a purpose that goes deeper and is tied to the eternal purposes of God. To surrender to that call is the first step on the path to a more satisfactory purpose.

The journey to destiny takes many paths. Read the stories of great leaders (many who, to all appearances, were unremarkable until some defining moment) and you will discover that there may have been just a few choices that put them on the track to fulfilling a singular purpose in their lifetime.

Many of us go through life so preoccupied and busy with the unimportant that we are unable to see much beyond the fast track to success or the pursuit of retirement. Discovering purpose is not so much a process of growth as it is an awareness of what is truly important. Life can overrun your purpose if you let it. It is never too late, however, to discover and renew purpose, vision, and strategy for your remaining years.

⋯> IMPACT

It takes some digging through the layers of life to find the purpose God has placed in us. Find it. Surrender to it. The goal is to live intentionally, not reactively. The goal is to fulfill God's idea of success.

What direction have I received from God and not followed? Why didn't I?

What sense of calling, purpose, or destiny is in my heart now that I need to pursue?

What three specific things do I need to change?
What are three things I can start doing now?

_____

_____

_____

_____

_____

_____

_____

_____

_____

_____

_____

_____

"No matter what your biological heritage—good or bad—the love of God for you is your inheritance."

CHAPTER 8

I YAM
WHAT I YAM

Embrace Your Heritage

···> IDENTITY

When I went to the University of Minnesota to live on the campus in an apartment with two other guys, it was the first time I had lived apart from my family. We were all Christians, with a desire to do the right things in life, but from very different backgrounds. Perhaps for the first time, I realized what an unusual and special family I had.

Both of my roommates had grown up in dysfunctional homes, and they lived with the consequences of that life nearly every day. To go home for the weekend was not a pleasure but a burden. They were making choices to break the patterns that were so much a part of their families, but it wasn't easy. They were nice guys with a lot of baggage.

One evening I was alone in our apartment. The reality of a family crisis for one of my roommates had hit us hard the day before. I was quietly working around the house when I spontaneously began to thank the Lord for the family I had. I had never before experienced such a depth of gratitude. A sense of thanksgiving swept over me. Tears were literally dripping into the sink as I washed the dishes. It finally became so strong that I had to stop and kneel by my bed, naming people and circumstances for which I was thankful.

It was an amazing thirty minutes that brought into focus
for me the tremendous gift I had been given. That sense of
gratitude and favor has never left me.

···> INTEGRITY

Lord, you have assigned me my portion and my cup;
you have made my lot secure.
The boundary lines have fallen for me in pleasant places;
surely I have a delightful inheritance.
I will praise the Lord, who counsels me;
even at night my heart instructs me.

PSALM 16:5–7

In Psalm 16:2, David wrote, "You are my Lord; apart from
You I have no good thing." David had come to understand
that as good as his family was, as favored as they might be,
apart from the Lord, he had nothing that was truly good.
In reality, he was not considered of significance in his
own home. When Samuel came to Jesse's home looking for
God's appointed man to lead Judah and Israel, David was
not even invited to appear. In some ways, he was considered
an outcast. Yet David was chosen to lead.

During that evening in my apartment, I gave my family back to the Lord. I laid my heritage at the foot of the cross. In a way, I died to all that I had received, and I prayed, "God I want my inheritance to come from You. I look to You alone."

IMPACT

No matter what your biological heritage, good or bad, the love of God for you is your inheritance. You are what you are. Embrace your heritage and every experience of life. Bring it all to Jesus. Rejoice in it, be grateful for it, find delight in it, and glean from it. He is able to take every part of our past, every pain and sorrow, every bit of brokenness and bring redemption and wholeness. When God becomes our source and our inheritance, then every part of our heritage becomes fuel for redemption and healing to others. In fact it is through our need that He is able to bring hope and life.

What experiences most strongly shaped my sense of identity as a child?

Who were the most powerful examples of love as I was growing up?

How have I seen God's redemptive love bring healing where there once was pain?

_____

_____

_____

_____

_____

_____

_____

_____

_____

_____

_____

_____

_____

"There is a liberation that comes when we finally grasp that we are completely undeserving of the mercy and love of God—and yet He has given it anyway."

CHAPTER 9

WHEN THE LIMELIGHT FADES

Finding True Confidence

····> IDENTITY

After many years of leadership in a corporate setting, I went through a time of significant transition. I started a consulting business of my own. Abruptly, there was no title, no platform for influence, and little exposure to the many relationships that had defined my identity and impact. All of the public props were gone. I stopped getting a biweekly paycheck and I felt I was very much on my own.

Some of my initial business decisions didn't work out so well. This affected not just me but my whole family. My wife and I began to struggle in our relationship; cracks in our communication and decision-making were exposed. All of this deeply affected my identity as a man—my leadership at home, my security as a businessman who was now "consulting" with others, and my sense of confidence.

Living the Christian life and looking good is all pretty simple when we are going the same direction as everyone else. When all the external structures of life change, however, we are forced to dig much deeper to find where our confidence really lies.

I remember well the many times I poured my heart out to God, sought the counsel of dear friends, and spent hours in honest and vulnerable conversation with my wife. I started to realize that I didn't need to have position, title, public responsibility, or an impressive resume to have confidence. It is gained by loving and obeying God in the basic things of life, by whole-heartedly loving and caring for my wife, by being present in my kids' lives, and by working hard in whatever is before me. My future is in His hands whether the external structures and platforms are there or not.

⋯> INTEGRITY

Continue in him, so that when he appears we may be confident and unashamed before him at his coming.... This then is how we know that we belong to the truth, and how we set our hearts at rest in his presence whenever our hearts condemn us. For God is greater than our hearts, and he knows everything. Dear friends, if our hearts do not condemn us, we have confidence before God and receive from him anything we ask, because we obey his commands and do what pleases him.

1 JOHN 2:28; 3:19-22

It is a wonderful thing when we discover our own unworthiness. There is a liberation that comes when we finally grasp that we are completely undeserving of the mercy and love of God and yet He has given it anyway. To realize that "God is greater than our hearts and He knows everything" creates freedom. Though I had accepted the forgiveness and cleansing of Jesus' love early in life, I began to understand in a new way that my hope and confidence could not be built on my performance. It had to be established in the truth that God loves me, that He knows everything about me, and wants me to have my "heart at rest in His presence."

Through these trials, I discovered a sense of calm trust in God's provision—an ability to "continue in Him." It is not that there were no financial challenges or times of uncertainty. But in a deep way, in many areas of life, my heart found rest. I wanted to live God's way, in His timing, and doing His will. It is beyond explanation how the peace of God begins to rule in our hearts and strengthen our character when we let Him be our confidence. However, I can tell you it changes everything.

···> IMPACT

We may rely on all kinds of accolades, commendations, and references as a basis for confidence. The starting place of confidence, though, is found in transparency and humility before God and those closest to us. Don't underestimate the significance of walking a simple life of humility, love, and service to your family. Leaving the limelight to find the true Light brings a confidence that cannot be shaken.

What external structures, systems, and supports give me confidence today?

In what ways can I begin to shift my confidence to God's love and my life "in" Jesus?

Where do I need to walk in new transparency, humility, and simplicity with God and those closest to me?

_____

_____

_____

_____

_____

_____

_____

_____

"Fully embracing God's calling and authority can be as simple as reaching into the lives of people right next to you."

CHAPTER 10

EMBRACE
YOUR HIDDEN
LEADER

Find Identity Right Where You Are

···> IDENTITY

Ken, his wife, and their three children in many ways resembled a typical suburban family. He had served as a missionary in Indonesia, but now he was "home" and consulting in the computer technology industry. His problem was, having once served in a "ministry" role, being in the business world now just didn't feel right. He told me, "I did not like the feeling of being a 'failure' and felt guilty for letting down the people who had 'higher' hopes for me."

Over time, however, the Lord began to reveal a legitimate and essential purpose in His plan for Ken—to be "light and salt" in a world that sorely needed it. He often found himself in "dark places" as the sole Christian in work environments that were hostile to the gospel. He became aware of opportunities in which he could affect change in the culture of his organization. At times he was simply "there" for a person going through personal or professional loss or change.

Ken daily interacted with people who had no other contact with believers, in relationships that no pastor or other professional religious person could ever establish, and with people who would not set foot in a church. In his words, "These are people for whom Jesus died! How else would they be reached unless I, personally, reached them? Viewed like this, simply 'working' can be a noble calling— a calling that can change the world as much as being a full-time missionary."

···> INTEGRITY

So from now on we regard no one from a worldly point of view. Though we once regarded Christ in this way, we do so no longer. Therefore, if any one is in Christ, he is a new creation; the old has gone, the new has come! All this is from God, who reconciled us to himself through Christ and gave us the ministry of reconciliation: that God was reconciling the world to himself in Christ, not counting men's sins against them. And he has committed to us the message of reconciliation. We are therefore Christ's ambassadors, as though God were making his appeal through us. We implore you on Christ's behalf: Be reconciled to God. God made him who had no sin to be sin for us, so that in him we might become the righteousness of God.

2 CORINTHIANS 5:16–21

God's desire and purpose has always been that we live in relationship with Him and live as His agents in this world. As we find our personal place in His purpose, a clear sense of personal destiny and calling will guide and influence everything we do. We will see the world with a new perspective, through different lenses. Personal purpose and significance is found in the heart of God—"reconciling the world to himself in Christ." He wants us to join Him in this overarching task.

As the body of Christ, and under His leadership, we are called to work together as the church. The only way we are going to "reconcile the world" to Christ is to embrace and engage in the networks of relationships that we have. Please know that God has given you authority to "go" to your Jerusalem as well as the remotest places of the earth. His purpose includes both.

⋯⋗ IMPACT

Fully embracing God's calling and authority can be as simple as reaching into the lives of people right next to you. Many do not know a real Christian. They only know stereotypes. The place you are today and the work you do there puts you in a unique and powerful position to demonstrate the transforming love of Christ to people who may be in places where "darkness reigns." Is your "hidden leader" ready to come out?

Leadership is knowing the destination and taking others with you. It is rooted in following Jesus in what He is already doing for us. As we follow Him, we lead others.

Who are the people in my sphere of relationship and responsibility that I could reach and love?

What keeps me or holds me back from taking a risk to express God's love and serve as a "minister of reconciliation"?

How can I begin to connect with those in my circle of relationships?

_____

_____

_____

_____

_____

_____

_____

_____

_____

_____

*"God shows us the way,
but it is up to us to do the
work and to pay attention to
the condition of our hearts."*

CHAPTER 11

CLEANING OUT THE CLOGS

Clear and Guard Your Heart

···> IDENTITY

A particular town was known for its health, for the beauty of its gardens, and for the freshness of the many ponds and streams that flowed through its parks.

In this town there was one peculiar character, an old man. He would disappear for hours, heading off into the forest and up into the hills or into one of the parks. One morning the local constable found the old man dead. News of his death spread quickly throughout the town, but there were few who cared or really stopped to think about the passing of the old man.

The next summer, the town's people began to notice something odd. There was a bit of an odor in the air, the streams did not run quite as full, and the ponds and lakes began to grow much more algae. They could not recall this ever happening before. Another summer came, and the streams turned to a trickle, the ponds and lakes grew muddy and green, and the park gardens no longer bloomed. Sadness crept over this once lovely old town.

It was during this summer that a young lad of 15 began to wander in the hills surrounding the town. He remembered the old man he used to follow occasionally into the forests. He sought out the trail that the old man used to take. It had become overgrown with grasses and thistles in the two summers since the old man had died. Following the trail, though, the boy found an amazing maze of marshlands, streams, ponds, and springs that fed the streams. He also found that now the water outlets were blocked with leaves and debris.

The young boy trampled through and began to clear away debris that had piled up. The water began to flow. As he worked, he began to think about the old man. Is this where he went sometimes for days at a time? Was it his death that caused the change in the town?

No one knew exactly when the town began to come back to life, but some time during the summer, the streams and rivers began to flow more swiftly and purely. The boy knew that the old man had faithfully tended the secret source of the town's health. And now he knew his calling; he knew his task. This secret place was the "wellspring of life" for his town, and now it was his duty to care for it.

···> INTEGRITY

Above all else, guard your heart,
for it is the wellspring of life.

PROVERBS 4:23

It is the desire of Jesus to be the source of life in us from which all life flows. But the condition of of our outward life—the part that everyone sees—is influenced by the condition of our hearts.

There are a few key types of "debris" that can block our hearts. Unforgiveness dams up the human heart and blocks the flow of life. Disrespect hinders our prayers, shatters the spirit, and closes our understanding to the needs of others. Unconfessed sin breeds fear and darkness. Darkness fosters secrets, binds freedom, and robs confidence.

If this spiritual debris is neglected and allowed to clog up our hearts, we become hardened and dry. The Spirit of God is not able to truly flow through us. Not only do we become stagnant, but our stagnation affects growth in those closest to us. The only solution is to clean out the clogs and keep the passageways clear. God shows us the way, but it is up to us to do the work.

···> IMPACT

Pay attention to the condition of your heart. Make time to "pour out your heart" before God! Walk in the light. Make relationships right. By investing the time to keep communication and love open and flowing, we feed the gardens of the soul.

Are there people whom I have not forgiven? How can I remove that clog?

Am I walking in openness, respect, and care with my spouse? If not, what debris do I need to clear out of our relationship?

What steps should I take to "walk in the light," to take what was wrong and make it right?

_____

_____

_____

_____

_____

_____

_____

"Following God's lead is not so much about charting a precise course on a map, but rather using a compass to navigate through the storms and tests of life one at a time."

CHAPTER 12

EATING AN ELEPHANT

*Biblical Leadership
One Step at a Time*

····> IDENTITY

At the height of my career, I had a growing sense of uneasiness that lasted for a number of months. As leadership responsibilities grew in one area, pressures were growing in others. My family was getting bigger and requiring more time and attention. There are times when it is absolutely necessary to streamline life. This was one of those times.

I was feeling that change was coming and I needed to prepare for it. There was no looming decision. There were no offers on the table. I was not dissatisfied with what I was doing, I just had a growing uneasiness with the status quo. I felt I was on a collision course with a new future.

One of the key decisions I made during this time was to grow in understanding of the biblical perspective of leadership. I dived into a two-year journey through the lives of great men in the Bible. I wanted to know how God worked in their lives, how He prepared them for what He had in mind. I found that at the core of every one of these "heroes of the faith" was a clear and undeniable posture before God. They looked to Him as Master of every aspect of life, they trusted Him to be their provider and sustainer, and they invited Him to live within them.

My study led me to some foundational choices that became stakes in the ground—points of reference for decisions, attitudes, and actions. If I was going to realign my life, I needed to do it right—one bite at a time if necessary—until I was following God's plan, not my own. I had to change the way I made decisions, my attitudes about those decisions, and ultimately my actions.

INTEGRITY

Similarly, encourage the young men to be self-controlled. In everything set them an example by doing what is good. In your teaching show integrity, seriousness and soundness of speech that cannot be condemned.

TITUS 2:6-8

There were a few common nonnegotiables I found repeated in the lives of the leaders and heroes of the faith I studied. Things that were simple but absolutely necessary for their walk with Christ. Following their example was a tall order to obey. But when I digested these truths one by one, I found my attitudes and actions started to change.

Persevere in tribulation. In John 16:33, Jesus said to His disciples, "In the world you will have tribulation" (ESV). He was letting them know that life would not be easy; but, there is a fruit of character that comes as we persevere.

Be faithful in responsibilities. Joseph, the favored son who was sold as a slave by his brothers, was faithful in whatever responsibilities he was given—whether as a slave, a prisoner, or as second in command in the land of Egypt. It was a daily choice to be faithful—to finish each responsibility well. It really doesn't matter how many responsibilities we carry; being unfaithful is not an option. Faithfulness requires that we either complete the responsibility with excellence, get help, or transfer the responsibility to someone else capable. It is not wrong to admit inability to fulfill something, but it is not okay to walk away irresponsibly.

Love and embrace truth. One of the most liberating choices in life is to walk fully in light and in truth. It isn't until we embrace truth that the fear of man is driven out of our lives and new authority and peace takes its place. As Jesus stood before Pilate, He was being questioned about why the Jews were so viciously angry with Him. In the midst of the questioning, Jesus stated, "To this end was I born, and for this cause came I into the world, that I should bear witness unto the truth" (John 18:37 KJV). His stand for truth would kill Him. Our stand for truth brings life.

The paths laid out by these great men helped me to streamline life and protect those under my leadership when tougher times did come.

··> # IMPACT

If, as the saying goes, you can eat an elephant one bite at a time, then streamlining your life can be done one persevering, faithful, truth-filled step at a time. I am convinced that when we follow the examples of the men and women of faith, we will come to a place of absolute reliance on God's will and word for the future.

Is there tribulation and trouble in which I need to endure and persevere?

What responsibilities have I taken on that I need to finish well or transition to someone else?

Is there truth about me that I have been refusing to embrace?

_____

_____

_____

_____

_____

_____

*"Saying no to some choices
so we can say yes to others helps
us prioritize what really matters
and helps us define our purpose
and calling."*

CHAPTER 13

THE PLIGHT OF THE "YES MAN"

Learning the Value of No

···> IDENTITY

A friend of mine hosted a couple of newcomers from
Eastern Europe. They had for many years lived on a
subsistence standard of living. Their food was simple, their
selection sparse, and their finances barely kept them alive.
They were given the opportunity to come to the United
States to start a new life, and they jumped at it.

Shortly after arriving they went to a supermarket to
grocery shop. The selection and varieties in the cereal aisle
became so overwhelming that the woman went into shock
right there in the store. She was revived quickly, but it was
clear to my friend that more time was needed to introduce
these immigrants to the abundance of choices we have come
to take for granted.

We have become anesthetized by the plethora of options
offered to us daily. In some sense we live in shock. We have
almost stopped truly choosing and have become addicts
of choice—choosing everything we possibly can. Our
discernment has eroded. It's seems we've all become "yes
men." We say yes to more food, more obligations, more
possessions. When is enough, enough?

···> # INTEGRITY

Therefore, since we are surrounded by such a great cloud of witnesses, let us throw off everything that hinders and the sin that so easily entangles, and let us run with perseverance the race marked our for us. Let us fix our eyes on Jesus, the author and perfecter of our faith, who for the joy set before him endured the cross, scorning its shame, and sat down at the right hand of the throne of God.

HEBREWS 12:1-2

The greatest discipline is saying no to what is not essential to fulfilling the vision and purpose in our lives. Until it becomes a life or death issue, we tend not to make the hard decisions. We keep thinking that we can make it work. So, we say yes to everything. "Yes," we can juggle all the balls, spin all the plates, and pursue all of our dreams. It is when surviving becomes the issue that we are finally forced to say no.

Ernest Shackleton, the English explorer, attempted to cross Antarctica in 1914. Within weeks of beginning his quest, his ship, the *Endurance*, froze fast in an ice flow ending any chance of accomplishing his original dream. He had to say no to his initial vision in order to say yes to a higher purpose—to get all twenty-seven of his men safely back to civilization. As hopes were literally smashed (the Endurance was crushed and sunk by the ice), he continually had to realign his priorities so his crew could survive the brutal Antarctic conditions for just another month, a week, or at times, simply one more day.

All of this culminated in an incredible journey, an 850-mile trek over some of the most treacherous seas in the world. His leadership under the strain of unbelievable conditions resulted in all of his crew surviving the ordeal. The accomplishment is almost beyond belief.

Their extreme conditions and constant battle for immediate physical survival made it easier to make adjustments in their actions. It may be more difficult for us to recognize the threats of death in our own lives, and therefore we may be less willing to make the hard choices. It is easy to say no to material things when they could literally be the weight that brings our death. It is much harder to say no to a promotion, a bigger house, or a better car.

We are running a race—one that requires endurance and perseverance. Jesus, our leader, was willing to lay down His life to make a way for us to know the Father. We are called to lay aside anything that hinders running this race.

···> IMPACT

If we do not honestly deal with the implications of saying
yes all the time, we may not be able to accomplish God's
highest calling. Saying no to some choices so we can say yes
to others helps us prioritize what really matters and helps
us define our purpose and calling. You never know who
may be watching or even depending on your choices.

*What do I hold onto that hinders and entangles me from fulfilling the vital
purpose and vision I hold?*

*Is there an area where I am not being honest about the drain and drag of
things I hold on to?*

How can I get unentangled to focus on what is most essential?

_____

_____

_____

_____

_____

_____

"God is not timid with His children. He cuts away what does not bear fruit and prunes what does so that it will bear more."

CHAPTER 14

HOW DOES YOUR GARDEN GROW?

Pruning for Impact

···> IDENTITY

After more than twenty-four years in corporate business roles, my career changed drastically. God led me out of the world I had known so well into a world I hardly knew at all. The clear and predictable world was replaced by one of uncertainty and discovery. God was forcing me to learn to trust Him all over again.

I knew when I left the corporate environment that I would not be returning to that comfortable world. Therefore, in my own wisdom, I began to figure out my new role. Oh, I prayed and asked God for guidance, but I also forced ideas, partnerships, and investments. It was my attempt to do something significant—to forge my own way. I lost money, strained close friendships, and wasted precious time with each "failed" effort.

When the pressure of these decisions began to affect our home, God reduced (pruned) me to a very simple approach to life: find my place and identity in Him no matter what other people think.

I remember praying at some point in this process, "God, I don't need to be significant, no one needs to know where I am or what I am doing, and if You have something more for me to do, I leave that to You. I commit to being faithful in what is here, right now." That moment of surrender produced a desire in me to be content to love and be loved by my Father in heaven, to love and care for my wife and family, to work hard on what is in front of me, and to just be faithful.

···> INTEGRITY

I am the true vine, and my Father is the gardener. He cuts off every branch in me that bears no fruit, while every branch that does bear fruit he prunes so that it will be even more fruitful.

JOHN 15:1–2

I once watched a horticulturist prune (or "nearly destroy") shrubs and flowering plants in the name of healthier and more productive plants for the future. Now, I tend to hesitantly, gingerly trim a shrub for fear of damaging or killing it; however, I am not a horticulturist. God is. He is not timid with His children. He cuts away what does not bear fruit and prunes what does so that it will bear more. God did some heavy-duty pruning in my life and relationships. He pruned away my sense of identity so I was no longer wrapped up in what I was doing and what others thought about me. My confidence in what I could see and touch was cut away. Independence and self-reliance, fear of failure and loss, my picture of the future, and my ambition were stripped away. They were replaced with a willingness to risk all and trust God completely to receive what He had in mind for my family and me. I am convinced that this pruning was not just for me, but also for the welfare of my family and ultimately for others in my sphere of influence. Where there had been stress over finances, we came to a place of trust and rest. When there was concern over where the next job would come from in the consulting business, there was knowledge that God was leading and opening doors. We really discovered, in a new way, that our future was in God's hands. His pruning helped us to grow and made us fruitful.

···> IMPACT

Left alone, a plant will become overgrown. It may look impressive, but the reality is that its fruit is worthless. Pruned, the plant will bear fruit that is sweet to the taste and desirable. We all want the fruit of our lives to be like that, to give life to others.

In what ways has pruning taken place in my life?

What fears and concerns or points of identity still hold me back from surrendering to God's care and work in my life?

Is there something or some way that I can begin to trust God more fully?

_____

_____

_____

_____

_____

_____

_____

_____

_____

_____

_____

_____

_____

"God's call on our lives means leaving behind the person we were. It means taking Him by the hand and losing ourselves in Him—wherever that leads."

CHAPTER 15

LOSE YOURSELF

Following God's Leading

⋯> IDENTITY

After sixteen years in the same town, my wife and I made the decision to move. Everything about moving was hard. Our four children had all been born there. We all had close relationships and work connections. The children had friends and school ties.

The time came to let our 13-year-old daughter know of our upcoming move from Arkansas to Colorado. As Danielle quietly listened, her eyes filled with tears. Finally, out of her sad silence, she said, "I'm going to lose my friend Megan, my friends at school, my cousins, my grandpa and grandma, my friends at church...I am going to lose myself."

There are statements that burn into your soul and mind, and this was one of them. In a profound way, she had named all those who defined her identity. They were the "mirrors" in which she saw herself.

A few days earlier, I had read the words of Jesus in which He listed the many relationships that hold our love. He said, "Whoever finds his life [self] will lose it, and whoever loses his life [self] for my sake will find it" (Matthew 10:39). Danielle was about to lose her self, and it hurt deeply. But in my heart I believed the promise that Jesus gave: "Whoever loses his life for my sake will find it."

Four years after our traumatic move, Danielle and I drove to a school event where she was going to spend an evening with friends. We discussed the conversation from four years earlier. Danielle exclaimed, "I've found so much more than I lost." The promise was true. My daughter had grown from a person defined by others to someone who was finding strength, purpose, contentment, and confidence from who she was in Christ—from the inside out.

···> INTEGRITY

Anyone who does not take his cross and follow me is not worthy of me. Whoever finds his life will lose it, and whoever loses his life for my sake will find it.

MATTHEW 10:38–39

Fear of letting things go, things that have defined our identity, often stops us from making changes for the better. If our identity is dependent on outside sources or on others, then when our world shakes (and it will shake), we are shaken, too. Integrity is built when pressure comes. It is proved when the shaking challenges us to trust.

After the children of Israel had escaped from 450 years of slavery in Egypt, they began to grumble and complain. Once the difficult journey across the desert became a reality, they demanded, "Let us go back to Egypt!" They would rather have lived a predictable life of slavery and oppression than walk the journey of risk and freedom. When change comes, it is tough to lay down the comforts of where we are, the security of those we know, and the confidence of routine, even when these things actually represent bondage. It is even more difficult to leave something sweet and wonderful for a new future, which is what my family experienced.

God's call on our lives means leaving behind the person we were. It means taking Him by the hand and losing ourselves in Him—wherever that leads.

···> IMPACT

When we entrust our identity to Jesus Christ, we find a new future and life. It may stretch us, but we also gain strength and depth of character. When God calls us to a new place, we have the confidence to go. He is faithful.

Where am I entrusting my security? Is it in things and people or in God himself?

Where have I attached my affections? What can I do to change the focus of my affections?

Have I surrendered and released all of the loves of my life, all of the relationships and activities that define me?

_____

_____

_____

_____

_____

_____

_____

_____

_____

_____

_____

_____

"Crises are gifts from God."

CHAPTER 16

CLIMBING OUT OF THE MUD HOLE

*Overcoming the Chilling
Realities of Life*

⋯> IDENTITY

I remember the day when the two owners of DaySpring Cards and I sat in the small conference room between their offices and realized that we were in serious trouble. In fact, I remember more than I'd like of the soberness in their faces...of the ponderous weight of the silence after the financial realities we were facing had been discussed. I remember the solemn realization of just how grave the situation was—it was highly doubtful we could produce enough sales to stay in business for another year.

On that day, the grim and chilling reality of being seriously stuck in a "mud hole" was forcing us to take an honest and soul-searching look at what to do next. Turning back was not an option. Slow death wasn't either. We knew we had to go forward, but the how and where eluded us.

In order to climb out of the mud, in order to survive, doing more of the same wouldn't work. Sheer willpower and personal effort were not enough this time. We needed help. So where does one's confidence and perseverance come from during trying times?

···> # INTEGRITY

So do not throw away your confidence; it will be richly rewarded.
You need to persevere so that when you have done the will of God,
you will receive what he has promised. For in just a very little while,

   "He who is coming will come and will not delay.
   But my righteous one will live by faith.
   And if he shrinks back,
   I will not be pleased with him."

But we are not of those who shrink back and are destroyed, but of
those who believe and are saved.

HEBREWS 10:35-39

You can't help but identify deeply with what you do and the
impact of that effort. There was no question that all of our
identities had been shaped by our work together. Failure
would shake our confidence deeply. Not only that, but we
were responsible for sixty employees, nineteen of whom had
uprooted their lives and families to move from Southern
California to Northwest Arkansas to join our team.

We knew God had led us to where we were. We were
committed to those who were looking to us to lead. And we

believed in the future of DaySpring. We could not shrink back in our crisis. We had to face it and know we were doing the right thing.

Integrity demanded that we make some hard choices. We had to lay aside our egos, let go of what wasn't absolutely critical to our core mission, and invest in what would get us out of this hole. We couldn't pander to our sense of loss or pain.

Over the next several months, we let go of things we loved, things that had drained our resources, and focused on what would make the biggest impact and contribution. We threw our full effort and commitment in that direction. There was no room for the pet projects or programs.

We had to face it and know we were doing the right thing. We persevered. Everything had to be kept practical and proactive. This crisis became a turning point for DaySpring. From that point on, the company was able to grow and reach out in ways we had never imagined. When I look back at this "mud hole," I know that it changed the company and it changed us into something better than we were.

···> IMPACT

Crises are gifts from God. If we will do the right thing
and persevere, character is forged. Each person must find
a way out of their unique "mud hole." That process creates
desperation for God and a pursuit that leads to trusting
Him more completely.

*If I am in my own "mud hole," what are the chilling realities—the cold
hard facts—of my situation?*

*Who is in this "mud hole" with me? How can we come together to walk
through this difficulty and crisis?*

*What must I let go of? Where must I focus my energy and efforts to make
the greatest difference and impact?*

"This trimming away, no matter how difficult, compels us to live so dependent on God that we don't have the opportunity to rely on our own importance or success."

CHAPTER 17

GROWING GRAPES

Embracing God's Pruning

····> IDENTITY

My first task as team leader at Bethany International was
to evaluate our mission and its effectiveness. We needed to
formulate a new course of action based on our findings.
During one planning session, I drew two circles on the
white board. One said "Sending" and the other "Training."
Those were the two critical priorities of our mission and
vision, and had been for more than sixty years.

We then discussed the values and capabilities that had
been at the heart of Bethany's mission. After listing a
dozen components that had been a part of our organization
through the years, one by one, we removed all of the key
elements of Bethany's operating model and history. The
businesses, the campus and mission community, our
training, our global relationships...literally, all were either
radically altered or gone—nothing remained unscathed.

In the middle of all of this, I had a flash of realization.
In my own mind, I asked God a question: *Did You plan this?
Did You plan to remove all of these dear parts of our history, heritage,
and model?* I cannot say that He had done what seemed so
devastating and so painful, but I can say He had not left us.
He was at work to bring His good purposes to light. I was

convinced that God was committed to fulfill His purposes through us—if we would cooperate with Him.

During the next few months, I studied the idea of pruning and discovered an interesting fact: When growing grapes, the best fruit comes from one-year growth that is closest to the vine. This is not an insignificant fact. My natural tendency was to think in terms of measuring health of a vine through the abundance of branches and greenery. I discovered another fact: All the branches from one year's growth does not produce good fruit the next year. In other words, what was fruitful one year would not be fruitful the next.

···> # INTEGRITY

Every branch that does bear fruit he prunes, that it may bear more fruit.... And we know that for those who love God all things work together for good, for those who are called according to his purpose.

JOHN 15:2; ROMANS 8:28 ESV

It is our tendency to assume that bigger is better. We tend to think that the success of one year guarantees success for the next. We attach ourselves to the external appearances of fruitfulness and make formulas out of what worked yesterday. We tend to look at big homes, businesses, and churches and say, "There's success."

But at least in the growing of grapes, the cutting-back process must take place every year—the branches must be pruned all the way back to the vine every winter. It is the key to real fruitfulness. This trimming away, no matter how difficult, compels us to live so dependent on God that we don't have the opportunity to rely on our own importance or success.

I can say with certainty that when we embrace the pruning of God in our lives, no matter how it comes, no matter how painful it is, we will grow in *depth* of understanding of God's calling and ways. We will be "forced" to trust Him implicitly. And He will take us *further* than we could have dreamed.

As the Bethany team refocused on the core training and sending mission, we were able to adjust to the new realities. The pruning was painful, but through it a new vision and excitement emerged. After we went through the pruning, a visiting friend noted that the new energy and commitment was palpable on campus.

⋯⟩ IMPACT

Past success can be the biggest enemy of lasting impact. The temptation is to subtly shift from faith-in-God to faith-in-our-experience (our thinking, expertise, or position). In embracing God's pruning, we put our trust back in God and allow Him to work through us. Perhaps we aren't growing grapes, but accepting God's pruning in our lives might increase our output just the same.

Where has my attention shifted from relationship with God to things, other people, or myself?

How have I defined my future based on past successes? In what areas have I been unwilling to let go of the past (successes and failures)?

Am I willing to have only God as my source, to trust God that fully?

_____

_____

_____

_____

_____

"Compromise on the truth and you will be bound by lies."

CHAPTER 18

A LIE BY ANY OTHER NAME...

Follow Your Convictions

···> IDENTITY

We realized that the time had come to hire a CFO. The company was growing in sales and expanding product lines very quickly—frankly, it was stretching all of us. We agreed to hire our accountant for the job. He had been working for us through an accounting agency, knew our business well, would have a short learning curve, and was trusted by our leadership team.

A few months later, I began to notice that our profits seemed to be significantly lower each month than I would have projected. I asked the CFO to look into it. As we talked I remember noting that his upper lip was perspiring slightly, but I thought nothing of it at the time. He was facing a number of personal challenges. He said that he would look into the problem and get back to me.

A few weeks later Psalm 101 really caught my attention. "I will ponder the way that is blameless.... I will walk with integrity of heart within my house; I will not set before my eyes anything that is worthless.... A perverse heart shall be far from me; I will know nothing of evil" (vss. 2-4 ESV).

We eventually discovered that our CFO had been living a lie. Not only was his personal life in shambles, but he was the one who had been embezzling funds. He had set up duplicate supplier accounts in a nearby city, sent false invoices for product, and then authorized payment to these accounts. He was caught, convicted of interstate fraud and theft, and sentenced to serve prison time.

INTEGRITY

If you hold to my teaching, you are really my disciples. Then you will know the truth, and the truth will set you free.

JOHN 8:31–32

During one of the depositions, I asked that CFO why he had done it. He looked at me blankly and said that he did not know. Something had been compromised. Perhaps at first it was just a little compromise, but then it grew and became more bold and greedy until finally he betrayed people who truly trusted and cared for him. He had become fully immersed in a world that controlled him. Fear and greed ruled his life. There is always a point where living a lie begins to take over and control your life—he had passed that point.

The question Pilate asked Jesus is perhaps more relevant today than ever before: "What is truth?" Jesus had just said to him, "For this reason...I came into the world, to testify to the truth. Everyone on the side of truth listens to me" (John 18:37).

It is human nature to use words to deflect responsibility and guilt away from ourselves. Young children don't have to be taught how to lie; they are pretty good at it right from the beginning.

It was not in Jesus's nature to lie, deceive, or mince words. He spoke the truth, even when it meant His life. He lived without fear. He lived without greed. There was no selfish ambition in Him.

Alignment with truth—no matter what it costs us personally—is the only way to break the control cycles of fear and greed. In a world that compromises and rationalizes individual choices, those who are committed to walk in the light and uncompromising integrity will stand out.

⋯> IMPACT

We are called to be people of the truth. A friend of mine has a saying, "If you don't know the truth, you will not be able to recognize lies." We have watched presidents lie to the American people, we have seen sports and entertainment stars lie in the courtroom, and we have witnessed religious leaders compromise their witness for personal gain. No wonder our culture doubts its leaders. Compromise on the truth and you will be bound by lies. We need to be a people who will tell the truth.

Keep your word. Walk your talk. Model alignment between beliefs, words, and actions! It will be a rare and wonderful gift to your children, to your friends, to co-workers, and to a watching world.

Are there areas where I am making compromises?

Do I tell "white lies" and shrug it off?

What can I do right now to begin to rebuild a legacy of truthfulness and honesty—to give to those around me an example of integrity?

_____

_____

_____

_____

_____

"In a world where tolerance is just another word for compromising principles, it is more imperative than ever to know what you believe, to follow truth, and to be willing to stand firm."

CHAPTER 19

YOU CAN'T
MAKE ME

Staying True to Your Ethics

⋯⋆ IDENTITY

Ryan was handsome, talented, and "golden." He was a quick learner. His employer gave him more and more responsibility until he was running the entire operation. As time passed and other workers came to him asking for favors, he always acted in his employer's best interests and did the "right thing." He was trusted not just because of his abilities and successes, but also because he could not be turned from doing what was just, ethical, and right.

Eventually he was tested at a level he had never experienced. Another key member of the leadership team came to him asking for an unethical and immoral favor. This person had the power to end his career. To grant the favor would be wrong. To resist would be the end of his leadership position. Ryan knew what he needed to do. He refused the request (threat), and it cost him his career.

What Ryan walked away with was a clear conscience. He knew who he was—a child of God—and was not willing to compromise. In his heart of hearts, his confidence grew.

···> # INTEGRITY

Depart from evil, and do good;
seek peace, and pursue it.

PSALM 34:14 KJV

The famous Old Testament character, Joseph, had to face
his brothers who had previously sold him into slavery. The
world was against him, but he stayed true to his convictions.
In the midst of an opportunity to take revenge on those
who had mistreated him, he said, "It was not you who did
this, but God. What you intended for evil, God intended
for good" (Genesis 50:19-21 PARAPHRASE). He saw that
God had used hardship in his life not only to shape his
personal character but also to position him to bring
solutions to serious social and economic challenges. He
persevered in doing what was right even when it felt like he
was abandoned and no one saw or cared.

The apostle Paul minced no words. "Do not be misled:
'Bad company corrupts good character'" (I Corinthians
15:33). Several hundred years earlier, Solomon wrote, "Do
not make friends with a hot-tempered man, do not associate
with one easily angered, or you may learn his ways and get

yourself ensnared" (Proverbs 22:24-25). A core group of primary influencers—leaders, companions, friends and co-workers—who have authority, can speak truth, and have lived solid, moral, and ethical lives are the most powerful force in establishing your identity as a person of integrity. They ultimately influence what kind of impact you can have on the world. They rub off on you. They challenge you to keep going in the right direction and to keep making strong, honorable choices. These are people you can trust and who help you define a clear sense of right and wrong.

In a world where tolerance is just another word for compromising principles, it is more imperative than ever to know what you believe, to follow truth, and to be willing to stand firm. The choices we make over time build a reputation of trust and confidence or create doubt and caution. Our choices define us.

⋯> IMPACT

Ultimately the test of a choice comes down to whether or not we truly trust that God is involved in our lives. Does God see me? Does He know or care what I am facing? Will it matter what I do or with whom I associate? Don't underestimate the impact of your choices—we never know who else is watching, or what we are being prepared for. When it comes to your choices, no one can make them but you.

Have I made compromises in moral or ethical areas because I thought no one else was looking or would know?

What current "evil" do I need to run from?

Who are three "good" people that I need to learn from, associate with, or be accountable to?

_____

_____

_____

_____

_____

_____

_____

_____

_____

"We all, at one point or another, come to a place where our capacity and capability are stretched beyond our abilities and gifts."

CHAPTER 20

MAYDAY, MAYDAY, MAYDAY

Knowing When to Ask for Help

···> IDENTITY

When I got my first "real" job, I had a voracious appetite for more—more tasks, more responsibilities, more leadership, more everything. Then one day I realized that I was in over my head. There was more on my plate than I could handle. I remember clearly walking across the hall to my boss's office and asking for help. It's amazing how difficult that was. But it was clear that the timelines, the number of projects to be completed, and the complexities were more than I could handle. I admitted it. And he was more than willing to help.

When we are young, we think we can do anything (and everything). In a sense, we believe we are invincible. When I first began working, it never crossed my mind that I could not do something, and I was always willing to learn. But there was a day when I clearly saw that some things took a lot more energy and effort than others. There was something in my ego that just didn't want to confess to the need for help. Once I did, though, the help was there and the work got done.

We all, at one point or another, come to a place where our capacity and capability are stretched beyond our abilities and gifts. It is hard to let go of our own picture of the future or change our plans or admit that we don't know the answer. For me there was a way through, but it meant honestly asking for help and letting go of some of that pride. That is always the challenge.

··> INTEGRITY

Moses said to the Lord, "O LORD, I have never been eloquent, neither in the past nor since you have spoken to your servant. I am slow of speech and tongue." The LORD said to him..."Your brother, Aaron... will speak to the people for you, and it will be as if he were your mouth and as if you were God to him."

EXODUS 4:10–11, 14, 16

Integrity demands that I honestly make room for others and their gifts. It has been said that a chain is only as strong as its weakest link. And it is true. The unwillingness to ask for help ultimately reveals the weakness is our chain, the chink in our armor, and the flaw in our thinking. Therefore integrity is not just about me alone, but how I make room to join with others.

God met Moses at the burning bush and gave him the mission to free the Jewish nation from slavery. Moses had spent forty years leading sheep around the desert. The thought of confronting Pharaoh and demanding that he release nearly two million slaves caused an immediate sense of inadequacy. He recognized the weak link in his chain. He asked for help. God provided Aaron to speak for him. The help of his brother strengthened Moses' leadership.

Jesus recognized that the disciples needed help if they were to fulfill the task of making Him known in all the world. He promised the Holy Spirit would come alongside and help. They were to go and wait until this Helper from heaven came. They waited. Their ability to carry out Jesus' commands were taken to a whole new level and dimension by waiting. If the disciples had not been willing to wait, to receive, and to work together with God's provision, they would have failed.

He also taught them the power of unity. When He sent them out to minister He sent them in teams. He talked often of His dependence on the Father's will and ways. He would ask two or three of the disciples to come with Him to help with a particular task. His message was clear: we are more effective and stronger when we work together.

⋯> IMPACT

When we are honestly open to recognizing our need for help, to asking God and men for that help, and when we make room to work with others, we are strengthened. We are made more complete and can see impact beyond what we could ever do on our own.

In what areas do I need help?

What keeps me from asking for help?

How can I make room for others to contribute their gifts?

_____

_____

_____

_____

_____

_____

_____

_____

*"When we find our strength
and supply in God alone,
a dynamic is created in us
that helps us serve others."*

CHAPTER 21

WHAT'S THAT SMELL?

Clearing the Air by Serving Others

⋯> IDENTITY

I had the privilege as a young man to work for a great
leader. To his very core, Dean served others every chance he
could, even if he suffered for it. He would make every effort
to speak words of encouragement. He was equally generous
with his time and with his finances. It was not unusual
to see him rolling up his sleeves to pitch in—picking up a
shovel, helping unload a truck, or giving someone a needed
ride. But more than once people let Dean down. It was
at these times when I saw that he wasn't just "performing"
acts of service; being a servant was his very nature. He
would repeatedly give and give again—even when it wasn't
deserved. I know it disappointed him when beneficiaries
of his kindness didn't follow through with commitments
or refused to take responsibility. However, the example of
his servant heart continued to influence others. Watching
Dean changed my identity as a leader.

⋯> INTEGRITY

Freely you have received, freely give.

MATTHEW 10:8

Every person has a basic need for affirmation, security, growth, unconditional love, and acceptance. These human needs are targets of temptation by Satan. We are tempted to look for situations, opportunities, and people around us to meet our basic needs rather than finding our source with God. When we find our strength and supply in God alone, a dynamic is created in us that helps us serve others.

There are two people that I cannot get away from: myself and God. Psalm 139:7 asks the question, "Where can I flee from your presence?" He is always near, always wanting to meet us and walk with us. Unless I recognize God's love and ability to meet every need that I have, I will always be looking to meet my needs through others—constantly trying to feed self-interest and ambition. However, when He is at the center and in control, His infinite resource flows to me and through me to others. Instead of constantly being a taker of life from those around me, I can now be a giver of life to others.

A friend of mine once referred to one of our mutual friends as having the "stench of need." It was true. Every time you were around this person, you sensed his desire for some form of recognition and honor. Until one finds that source of love and approval from God, they look for it from others. They smother people with questions and shovel on flattery to anyone who will listen. It doesn't take long for the situation to really stink!

When our relationship is right with God, His power and love flows into us and then out of us into every other relationship. We are only able to give away what we have received—we do not have an infinite source of patience, wisdom, love, forgiveness, kindness, tenderness, joy, peace, or goodness. When that core relationship is balanced, it lays the foundation for living as a servant—for developing life-giving relationships.

···> # IMPACT

The starting point of service is to know and experience the undeserved love and acceptance of God. In Jesus our greatest needs are met. While we were sinners, before we had done anything to earn His love. Even when we had the "stench of need," He loved us and gave His life for us. It is from this place of unconditional love that we begin the journey of serving others.

What are some areas in which I have received much? How can I serve in these areas?

Where do I draw my strength and life from? Do I draw it from God, or am I looking to others?

How can I express the servant heart of Jesus? Who are the people that I can begin to serve right now? How?

*"Knowing that I have
a significant place in
God's eternal plan gives
my life meaning."*

CHAPTER 22

A HIGHER PURPOSE

The Search for Meaning

···> IDENTITY

One day when my dad was in college, as he walked between classes, he heard in his mind, *Harold, you're going to teach.* As simple as that he realigned his life patterns to prepare for teaching. He read, studied, organized concepts, discovered illustrations, and served others with this one thing in mind.

My dad found meaning in his work on a daily basis. I remember when I was just a young boy watching him prepare for the next day of teaching. He prepared that way for nearly fifty-five years. Even now, when he is no longer able to teach publicly, he still has a daily routine of reviewing and organizing notes to convey some message or truth. He found great "satisfaction"; he was "happy in his work." Why? Because of meaning—his gift from God.

···> INTEGRITY

You received the Spirit of sonship. And by him we cry, "Abba, Father." The Spirit himself testifies with our spirit that we are God's children. Now if we are children, then we are heirs—heirs of God and co-heirs with Christ.

ROMANS 8:15–18

Saul, the Pharisee, was zealous for making sure that Christians were put in their place. He stood by as Stephen was stoned to death. He went from house to house throwing Christians into prison, and he was heading to Damascus to arrest more followers of Jesus. He was filled with purpose and had no question about what he was doing—until he had his Damascus Road experience.

Saul encountered Jesus on that road—a blinding light and then Jesus's voice speaking from heaven with instructions. This encounter realigned his purposes to those of God's so much that his name was changed to Paul. His purpose shifted from carrying out his own agenda to carrying out Jesus' agenda and purpose. For the next three years, Paul went into isolation to reorient his beliefs and thinking. When he emerged, he had a new identity of being "in Christ." His life, his position, his destiny, now found full expression in Jesus.

During a season of transition, after years of successful corporate leadership, a man in his early fifties was wrestling with life on a much smaller public platform. He was doing good stuff, but it was hard to see how it all fit into a bigger picture. What he did know is that God had directed him to work hard, live a simple life, and pay attention to his marriage and family. One day as he wrestled with the question of significance he prayed, "God, if no one knows I am here, or what I am doing, or even cares, if it is obedience to You, then I am okay with that—whether it ever changes or not." Finally he realized his purpose was to do the will of God, no matter what. It brought great peace and rest. A calling is not about significance in man's eyes, but obedience in God's eyes.

Knowing that I have a significant place in God's eternal plan gives my life meaning. We are already in the mind of our Creator. He knows us well and desires that we embrace the good works and calling that He has prepared for us. The apostle Paul went on to say, "That our God may count you worthy of his calling, and that by his power he may fulfill every good purpose of yours" (2 Thessalonians 1:11). Knowing this means that what I do—how I use my gifts—has a place in God's larger purpose. Jesus Himself said, "My food...is to do the will of him who sent me and to finish his work" (John 4:34).

⋯> IMPACT

Our future is bound to the purposes of Jesus and His eternal destiny. There is a depth of revelation that transforms our lives, unites us with the purposes and plans of Jesus, and brings fruitfulness to our lives.

How has God spoken to you and encouraged you in the past?

What is your sense of calling and purpose?
(This influences everything you do.)

How can you better align your priorities and life patterns to the calling of God in your life?

_____

_____

_____

_____

_____

_____

_____

_____

_____

_____

_____

_____

"The decision to respect others and to trust them is really not a showy symbolic event; it is a quiet release in the secret places of our hearts."

CHAPTER 23

ENOUGH IS ENOUGH

Giving Up the Need to Manage Others

···> IDENTITY

It was time for me to shift responsibilities to others. Our company had grown from a few dozen to nearly four hundred employees. The leadership team had stepped up to the challenge of growth in amazing ways. Each had, in their own way, made a unique impact into the culture and success of the company.

During this time, one particular manager needed to expand his leadership role. But, quite honestly, there were certain aspects of his leadership that I felt I needed to "manage." I often buffered his relationship with people throughout the company. He was more direct than I; he expressed his thoughts in stronger terms; his decision-making was more black and white. It was not that I was right and he was wrong, it was that we led differently, and I felt the need to direct his leadership.

···> INTEGRITY

As iron sharpens iron,
* so one man sharpens another.*

PROVERBS 27:17

Increasingly I became aware that I was standing in the way of his growth. I was not doing him, me, nor others in the company any favors by doing so. As I processed through what my response should be, Richard Foster's book *The Celebration of Discipline* provided a key piece of understanding: "The power of controlling others carries with it the anxiety of losing control, and the anxiety of being controlled by others.... We must forever give up our right to manage others."

My concern was that if I stepped out of the way and released more authority, things would get beyond my control—*he* would get beyond my control. What I had failed to realize is that men and women would more directly sharpen and shape him without my intervention. It required a release of control on my part, a giving up of my "right to manage others."

I made a significant decision while on the sun deck of a small cottage. There was no one else around, just me with my thoughts and a growing conviction that I needed to step out of the way. I decided to not hold so tightly to the reigns—to offer support without "taking over." The decision to respect others and to trust them is really not a showy symbolic event; it is a quiet release in the secret places of our hearts.

My dad once told me that he struggled with how to help people during a particularly stressful time. He was pouring out his questions to God. In the silence of the night he sensed God saying to him, "Harold, I work in the hearts of all the people, all the time." That is pretty amazing. We may be tempted to try to change or manage people when all the while God is working, teaching, loving, and disciplining them. Stepping out of the way allows God to work more fully.

···> IMPACT

After making the choice to step out of the way, I began to see how woefully inadequate my management of others truly had been. As the proverb says, "Like iron sharpens iron, so one man sharpens another." The leader that I had held back responded beautifully as he was more fully able to get feedback from other people in the company. They sharpened him, and he sharpened them. His abilities to see things clearly and to communicate directly increased the effectiveness of my own leadership. Stepping out of the way and releasing the gifts (and faults) of others expanded and grew our capacity.

In what ways do I control or manage people that may actually hinder growth and/or promote my own agenda?

What is it in me that I am afraid of losing or giving up?

How can I take steps to release others to both succeed and fail—trusting that they will grow?

_____

_____

_____

_____

_____

_____

_____

_____

_____

_____

_____

_____

"It is just when we begin to allow our identity to be shaped by the power entrusted to us that we become corrupted by it."

CHAPTER 24

THE POWER TRAP

Renewing a Right Spirit

····> IDENTITY

After ordering Uriah the Hittite to the frontlines of battle, King David gave the order for the troops to draw back so that Uriah would be killed and David could take his wife, Bathsheba. There is perhaps no more graphic portrayal of corrupted power than this picture. The prophet Nathan confronted David with a story of a rich man taking a prized young lamb from a poor shepherd so that he could serve it for a meal. David was devastated as he realized that he had done a very wicked thing.

David didn't get to this place of abuse of power and wickedness in one day. He had grown up as a shepherd. He was the last of Jesse's sons. God had selected David and had Samuel anoint him; God had given him great victories, a place of honor in Saul's court, the love of the Israelite people, and ultimately had raised him as king over all Israel and Judah. Somewhere along the line, the power, the fame, the honors began to creep into this humble shepherd's heart. He forgot his roots, which resulted in him committing murder and adultery.

···> INTEGRITY

Create in me a pure heart, O God,
and renew a steadfast spirit within me.

PSALMS 51:10

Power is part of life. It is not evil in and of itself. In fact, Psalm 62:11 says "that power belongs to God" (ESV). It flows from God. It is just when we begin to allow our identity to be shaped by the power entrusted to us that we become corrupted by it. A well-known quote sums it up succinctly: "Power corrupts; absolute power corrupts absolutely." As for David, pride, arrogance, using people, dominating others, impatience, and independence can override even the wisest counsel of those who care. It can happen anywhere—churches, work environments, homes. Power is given to serve, but when abused it always destroys.

David had allowed his right to rule others to be used for personal means. His power had corrupted his heart. His act had actually diminished his power—he lost a loyal citizen, refused the counsel of a trusted comrade, and damaged the kingdom. David's prayer of repentance was to return to a spirit of service.

David's identity as king of Israel and his power to act had become a "right" to him. He had forgotten his accountability to God, to those around him, and to those he led—his sheep. He had ceased being a shepherd; he had lost his identity as one who led and cared for those entrusted to him. He had somehow begun to serve his personal interests. Therefore, it wasn't enough for David to be forgiven; he needed to be renewed in the spirit of his heart. He needed to have wrong motives removed, hardness of heart made soft, and his actions corrected. God graciously met him and forgave his sin.

We could ask, "What good could come out of David's sin?" If David had not humbled himself and deeply repented of his sin, there would have been no redeeming value to us today. But he did. David turned his heart toward God; he sought the renewing of the "right spirit" that had so marked the character of his life. He also lost something, a loss that stands as a warning to us today—some of the innocence of a man who completely trusts God, some of the trust of his loyal men, and peace within his family. There are natural and logical consequences to our choices. It is God's goodness and mercy to forgive that restores us into a right relationship with Him—and gives grace for moving forward.

⋯> IMPACT

Beware of power that has been entrusted to you. Just when you start believing in your power over others, the spring is thrown and you are caught in a trap of your own making. Do not hold power as if it were owned by you, but treat it as if it were loaned to you for building up and serving others. Use the authority you have to build people up, not to tear them down.

How have I used my position or power for my personal purposes?

Who have I used to gain my desires? How have I hurt them?

In what ways can I make right what is wrong, turn from selfish motivations, and be renewed in a "right spirit"?

_____

_____

_____

_____

_____

_____

"Integrity is achieved when there is alignment between our beliefs, what we say, and our actions."

CHAPTER 25

WOBBLY WHEELS

Aligning Beliefs and Actions

···> IDENTITY

A friend of mine built a very successful organization. He gained notoriety on both a national and international level. In every way he seemed the ideal leader. I was proud of his success. He seemed to be doing a great job navigating the many responsibilities he was carrying. Over the years the accolades and recognition grew greater and more frequent. This guy was good.

What I couldn't know, however, was that he was struggling every day. The pressure was taking its toll on his emotional and personal life. Cracks under the surface were beginning to spread and show—cracks even those closest to him had not been aware of.

Then one day it all collapsed. In a painful moment, he left his position of leadership and had to face the crisis of his life falling apart and move in a very different direction. As I observed his pain and loss, I was challenged to inspect my own life. What was I hiding? Was I living honestly with myself and with others? If I was put under extreme pressure, would my tires stay on the road or would they blow out?

···> INTEGRITY

Consider it pure joy...whenever you face trials of many kinds,
because you know that the testing of our faith develops perseverance.
Perseverance must finish its work so that you may be mature and
complete, not lacking anything.

JAMES 1:2–4

The structural integrity of any item can only truly be
known when the stresses on that item are tested to the
extreme. For instance, an earthquake tests the structural
integrity of a building. The quality and balance of the
tires on your car are only fully exposed at high speeds. We
have all felt the shaking of a car with unbalanced tires or
seen the wear on tires that are not properly aligned. When
we are unbalanced in any area of life, it will become clear
under stress.

John Wooden, the legendary basketball coach at UCLA,
won ten NCAA national championships in twelve years.
He was a skillful coach who was able to develop teams that
could perform under pressure. He would work with his
players to run, pass, and play under severe pressure. Skill
that stands up under pressure—that is a priceless asset.

Integrity is achieved when there is alignment between our beliefs, what we say, and our actions. This type of alignment threatens even our enemies. It removes their opportunity for accusation, deceit, and corruption. Consistency and trustworthiness over time create a dependability that defines us.

Andy Stanley nailed it with this reality: "Your leadership can only go as far as your character will allow it." It was said of Joseph that he remained in prison and his dreams were not fulfilled "till the word of the LORD proved him true" (Psalm 105:19). When times were tough, he proved to be a man of tremendous integrity and character—worthy of being trusted.

⋯> IMPACT

We are told, "Testing proves and refines us—preparing us to faithfully fulfill our calling." An athlete or team who has been trained and tested in practice, who has been pressed to perform under pressure, and who has been coached in high stress situations will perform with confidence when the biggest game is on the line. They find a way to persevere and prevail—to move smoothly forward when others are showing signs of wobbly wheels.

Where is there a lack of alignment between what I say and what I do? Do I have a double standard?

What testing has come into my life and how have I responded to it? Have I run from that testing? Have I walked in accountability and humility?

How am I to persevere in current tests? What appropriate steps can I take to be faithful in the middle of trials?

_____

_____

_____

_____

_____

_____

_____

_____

_____

_____

_____

_____

_____

_____

_____

"When skill and integrity are successfully combined...they create a sustainable capacity to accomplish great purpose."

CHAPTER 26

STAND AND DELIVER

The Importance of Pairing
Passion with Skill

⋯> IDENTITY

Dave enjoyed leading the manufacturing branch of our company. He threw himself into every aspect of purchasing, quality assurance, workflow management, inventory control, and management. He continuously worked to improve and perfect work processes. One day he came to me and shared how critical and complex this world was becoming. Keeping up with the millions of transactions processed during the course of a week was no longer sustainable. If we didn't fix the problem soon, he confided, we were in for trouble.

I had a good understanding of what he was facing. I was personally familiar with manufacturing processes. I knew what we needed was passionate leadership in this area. I asked if he would like to provide the leadership needed for transforming and updating the manufacturing arm of the company. He responded positively. He immediately plunged into learning all he could—reading books, attending specialized training, searching out experts, and educating his team. His voracious appetite for knowledge and skill led to the transformation we required. He had the ability, the talent, and the passion. He acquired the skill.

···> INTEGRITY

Do you see a man skilled in his work?
He will stand before kings;
He will not stand before obscure men.

PROVERBS 22:29 ESV

Unfortunately, the church's emphasis on moral character
is not always paired with a priority of skill development.
Skill development is a necessity for a business to survive.
Conversely, the business world does not always put
adequate emphasis on the development of moral and
ethical integrity. When skill and integrity are successfully
combined, however, they create a sustainable capacity to
accomplish great purpose.

I recently met with a small organization struggling with
a financial crisis. The trouble was initiated when a good-
hearted man took over the financial books. He was a person
of impeccable character and honesty. Unfortunately, his
understanding of accounting and finances was not equal
to his good intentions. A few months after he took over,
the financial records were a mess and the organization was
struggling with cash flow. Good intentions are great, but

they are not enough—there must be skill development.

Integrity comes when good character and the right abilities and skills work together. God is interested in developing these in our lives. Moses had noble intentions to deliver the Israelites from slavery. God knew, however, that he would need to know the ways of survival in the desert between Egypt and the land of Canaan. So Moses, after fleeing from Egypt, spent forty years tending sheep and learning where water could be found. He became skillful in surviving in a dry and barren land.

⋯> IMPACT

Great responsibilities require superior skills. Moses went from tending sheep to demanding that Pharaoh let the Hebrew nation go free. David went from watching sheep to becoming king of Israel. There is no limit to the impact a single person with skill and passion can have on the world.

What talents do I have that have not been developed into skills?

What current responsibilities do I have that would be helped if my skills were further improved?

How can I invest in strengthening my skills and abilities? How can I help others grow in their capabilities?

_____

_____

_____

_____

_____

_____

_____

_____

_____

_____

_____

_____

_____

"Wisdom is knowing what to do and doing it; prudence is knowing what not to do and not doing it."

CHAPTER 27

HUGGING A SOFT PILLOW

Making Right Choices for Moral Leadership

⋯> IDENTITY

I remember as an older teen being in situations when I really considered doing something that I would later regret. The opportunity screamed at me to take action. No one was watching. No one would know. But I knew it was wrong. On one particular tempting occasion, it occurred to me that my dad would be deeply disappointed if he ever found out. Deep down I really did not want to shame my family. And that was enough to stop me.

Ken Lay, former CEO of Enron, professed, "I...lived my life in a certain way to make sure that I would never violate any law...certainly never any criminal laws...and always maintained that most important to me was my integrity, was my character, were my values." I first read this quote after he and many of the top executives of Enron were convicted of fraud, theft, and gross mismanagement of the company. They had deceived their employees, lied to shareholders, and grossly abused their power and the public's trust. Their careers ended in disgrace, their families were shamed, and their word and names were dragged through the dirt.

I wonder if at some time along the way—as they were making choices to defraud here, cover up there, and distort things elsewhere—if their consciences were pricked? Did they question their choices and actions? Based on the quote above, I suspect they ignored the warnings and plunged ahead.

It is easy to condemn the Enron executive team, and perhaps justifiably so. But how often do we compromise our ethics or morality—our integrity and our good character—in the name of "it's just a little thing?"

···> # INTEGRITY

The prudent see danger and take refuge,
but the simple keep going and suffer for it.

PROVERBS 27:12

Our choices establish and communicate our true values to others. What we say yes to, defines us. It builds the fence line that protects us from moral and ethical impurity or traps us on the wrong side. It becomes part of our identity and our voice to a watching world. We become known by our choices and actions.

Ethical conflict arises when we have confusion over who we are trying to please—God, other people, or ourselves? We always have a choice. Wisdom is knowing what to do and doing it; prudence is knowing what not to do and not doing it. Situations are put in front of us all the time, and we make choices to do them or not do them—going the speed limit, answering honestly, paying taxes, reporting income, gossiping about someone's failings, etc.

In processing our responses we ask questions such as: Would I want my children to know? Is it fair? Will I feel proud of this action? Does it compromise my reputation? Is it legal? Would I want my action posted on the Internet?

But the biggest question should be, when we have to give an account to God, will He be proud of this decision? Every person will be judged according to what he or she has done. There are no secrets.

⋯> IMPACT

A French Proverb says, "There is no pillow as soft as a clear conscience." We underestimate the power of right choices in shaping the identity of those around us. Even though I am now a husband and a father, I still remember the moments when I was confronted with moral and ethical decisions as a young man. My motivation in choosing came down to, "What would Dad say?" I am sure my children often wonder that as well. What would I say? I would tell them to hug tight to a soft pillow.

Have I compromised in moral and ethical areas?

What would have been the right thing to do?

How can I make right what is wrong?

_____

_____

_____

_____

_____

_____

_____

_____

_____

_____

_____

_____

_____

_____

"It is in the commitment to build a team and to grow the strength of that team where a leader ultimately finds completeness and identity in a band of comrades who work together for a common purpose."

CHAPTER 28

IT'S NOT ALL ABOUT ME

The Impact of a Team

⋯▷ IDENTITY

It's always a little dangerous, always a little risky, to ask for honest input from those you work with. After working with my leadership team for a dozen years, more or less, they knew me well. They responded to two specific questions I asked them: "What are the characteristics of the perfect boss?" and "Where do I need to improve?"

They confirmed the fact that I was *not* the perfect boss—I didn't define "success" as clearly as needed, didn't give enough feedback (good or bad), didn't bring adequate closure to an initiative, or run meetings productively. Even with my best intentions for the growth of others, I had avoided tough conversations, delayed giving praise, or took credit for something someone else had earned. But they were leaders who believed in me and leaders I believed in. We were a team.

Here's the point: it isn't about perfection. My success or failure did not rest on my abilities or weaknesses alone. It was about being a team, trusting each other, making room for the strengths of each person, and acting in agreement and accountability.

In fact, an honest assessment of team skills often makes the difference. It is in the commitment to build a team and to grow the strength of that team where a leader ultimately finds completeness and identity in a band of comrades who work together for a common purpose.

···> # INTEGRITY

Don't think of yourself more highly that you ought, but rather think of yourself with sober judgment, in accordance with the measure of faith God has given you. Just as each of us has one body with many members, and these members do not all have the same function, so in Christ we who are many form one body, and each member belongs to all the others.

ROMANS 12:3–5

When it came to His mission on earth, Jesus was constantly looking for ways to strengthen His team of disciples (followers). He never lost sight of the fact that one day He would physically leave earth and turn over execution of the big plan to those who had walked with Him for three and a half years. In His prayer just hours before He went to die on a Roman cross, He prayed, "My prayer is not for them alone. I pray also for those who will believe in me through their message" (John 17:20). He was staking the future on multiple generations of followers.

Jesus had mentored His disciples, coached them, developed their skills, provided clear feedback when they failed or doubted, and let them try things on their own. He was, in fact, the perfect boss.

He constantly trusted them to do more than they believed they could. He was not afraid to walk with them, to trust them, to send them out, or to identify with them in their failure. When they took initiative and began to serve people in His name, he encouraged and taught them ways to do better.

Jesus was committed to them...even when they weren't committed to Him...even when they failed. Integrity is to live true to the ideals, the standards, and the purpose of the team.

⋯> IMPACT

The twelve disciples went on to see thousands follow Jesus. They turned the Roman world upside down. They went throughout the known world and gave their lives just as their Master had done. One of the greatest compliments they received was from Jewish religious leaders who recognized these men as followers of Jesus. They were known by their mission, by how they modeled the same fearless love Jesus had shown, and how they spoke and moved under the authority of the Holy Spirit.

How am I known? Would others recognize that I follow Jesus?

Who am I following and how can I most effectively learn from them? What have I learned and how do I put it into practice?

Who is following me? How am I investing in their lives to succeed after I am gone?

_____

_____

_____

_____

_____

_____

_____

"The foolish man hears Jesus' words and does not do them. The wise man hears His words and does them. The difference is in the doing."

CHAPTER 29

CHOOSING
YOUR GURU

Who Should I Trust?

···> IDENTITY

At a particularly defining season in my life I had to make a central and strategic life decision. I had wrestled with priorities and choices for several months. There were plenty of pressures, responsibilities, and opportunities competing for my attention and time. I had to decide how to move forward—whom to trust, how much to give to God, which opportunities to choose.

I had seen diagrams of concentric circles showing God first, family second, church third, work fourth, and other commitments in the outer rings. It seems the further out from the center you get, the less critical the first priority often becomes. In a sense, these concentric circles create a hierarchy of need radiating from the "God" part of the circle.

The people of high influence in my life had placed God at the center of every aspect of their lives. God wasn't just a priority before everything, He was *in* everything. All relationships, responsibilities, and tasks were approached through the God circle. These people constantly sought to find what the Word of God might say about a decision, to sense the mind of the Spirit before proceeding, and to act or speak with a sense of ultimate accountability to God.

There was a "fear of the Lord" on their lives—a genuine sense of reverence and awe.

Everything they did, in every aspect of life, flowed out of their identity and relationship with Jesus and His Word.

⋯> INTEGRITY

The Spirit of the LORD will rest on him—
 the Spirit of wisdom and of understanding,
 the Spirit of counsel and of power,
 the Spirit of knowledge and of the fear of the LORD—
and he will delight in the fear of the LORD.

ISAIAH 11:2-3

Jesus walked on earth with an absolute dependence on the Holy Spirit to guide Him. He depended on the Holy Spirit in everything that He did. He taught, discerned, healed, confronted, comforted, decided, delivered, fed thousands, raised the dead, and turned water into wine in full reliance on the Holy Spirit. Even during His final breaths while hanging on the cross, He fully depended on and hoped in the Holy Spirit's power.

When looking for a guru, mentor, counselor, coach, or leader, seek out one who lives life in full dependence, surrender, and practical pursuit of God. One who loves the Word and makes all decisions in the light of what will honor and bring glory to Jesus. Although there are many skillful and capable people to provide input and give opinions in specific areas and disciplines of life, I continue to depend not on people who will just give an opinion, but on people who have followed Jesus.

So often these "gurus" refrain from giving advice and merely challenge me to dig deeper, to ask better questions, and let me know they believe in and trust me to do the right thing. They have called me to a higher standard and a life of honesty and integrity. They have impacted me greatly. As I have watched these people through the years, their dedication hasn't waivered or vacillated. Jesus has been their life, their Lord, and their provider and protector.

⋯> IMPACT

Jesus said that a foolish man is one who hears His words and does not do them. The wise man hears His words and does them. The difference is in the doing. But at the front end of this "formula" is listening. So often I have heard Jesus and His wisdom through the godly men and women in my life— people who have integrity and character, tested by the fires of life. Doing what God says will bear the fruit of wisdom and will help you become a wise voice for someone else.

Who are the people in my life that have placed Jesus in the center of every aspect of their life?

How can I listen, learn, and seek their counsel and input? In what ways can I make room for them to speak into my life?

In what ways can I steer a younger person toward godly leadership?

*"Jesus makes all things new
and more real than we have
ever imagined."*

CHAPTER 30

FURTHER UP AND FURTHER IN

Living With Eternity's Values in View

····> IDENTITY

When I was 17 years old, our family went for a vacation to a lake in northern Minnesota. We had three wonderful days of water sports, relaxing, playing ball, and eating. On the fourth day, August 6, 1969, the weather was hot and still. In the late afternoon, my 13-year-old brother and I had played ball with others at the resort.

Ours was one of two cabins on a small peninsula right at the water's edge. Late in the afternoon the air grew deathly still and then the winds begin to whip up. Other vacationers ran down the road toward us yelling "tornado!" As I looked to the southwest, all I could see was a giant dark cloud along the horizon. Our family ran into the nearest cabin, where seventeen people had gathered. I looked for my dad and saw him outside holding onto a tree. He was legally blind, though he could see shapes. The tree began to crack. I ran to my dad, and together we threw ourselves to the ground, clinging to each other.

During the next few seconds, all hell broke loose. The roar of the tornado as it passed over was deafening. In thirty seconds it was all over. As we rose from our small refuge, we were confronted with total devastation. All the trees had been uprooted or broken, cars were gone, and the cabin where my mom and brother had taken refuge was no longer on its footings. Everything was gone.

The lake was filled with debris. I began to look for any signs of life. At that moment I called out, "Jesus, Jesus," and immediately there came a peace—truly beyond understanding. A few heads began to pop out of the water, a couple of people climbed onto the shore perhaps one hundred yards from where the cabin had been. Then I saw my mom. She was alive but injured. But we never saw my brother Paul again.

INTEGRITY

I am the resurrection and the life. He who believes in me will live, even though he dies; and whoever lives and believes in me will never die. Do you believe this?

JOHN 11:25–26

These kinds of events shape our lives in both obvious and subtle ways. I immediately realized that I was living on borrowed time—my life was not my own. Our family would never be the same. Eternity was so much closer than it had ever seemed before. In the blur of watching my mom recover from the battering she had received and grieving the loss of my brother and six other friends, I also discovered the grace and goodness of God.

In the final book of the Narnia series, *The Last Battle*, C. S. Lewis entitled one of the last chapters "Further Up and Further In." In these final chapters, the characters are ushered through a stable door that represents the entrance to a more real world than they have ever seen or known. A world where "the inside is larger than the outside." And it is "more real and more beautiful than the Narnia outside the Stable door." It is the doorway to heaven.

Jesus makes all things new and more real than we have ever imagined. With this in mind, we are to go "further up and further in" in getting to know Him and all that He wants. It is a pursuit that will last for eternity and will grow sweeter as the ages pass.

···> IMPACT

My brother knew Jesus—or perhaps more accurately, knows Jesus. Even before he died, he was sensitive to heaven's reality. He had checked with each of us to see if we truly knew and trusted Jesus—He wanted to know if we would all be together someday. We will all give account to Jesus for the life we have led, whether we have trusted in His grace and lived with whole-hearted love for God. The impact of our lives is eternal. To go "further up and further in" in response to God's call is to live each day with eternity's values in view. We will impact others in more ways than we can measure.

Do heaven's eternal values and priorities hold first place in your heart?

Do you know beyond a doubt that Jesus is your resurrection and your life?

How can you respond today to the call to go "further up and further in"?

_____

_____

_____

_____

_____

_____

_____

_____